Mike Levy

About the Author

Mike Levy is a freelance author, journalist and press officer. He has several books to his credit including two for Law Pack (on presentations and stress management). He is working on a book on creativity in small organisations and one on effective meetings. He is planning to set up a consultancy offering mentoring to companies that are looking for innovative solutions and to encourage their organisation to be more creative. This company, Cambridge Creative Solutions, will be set up in the second half of 2002. Look out for www.cambridge-solutions.com.

As director of Key-Stage Company, he is also busy writing materials for schools using drama and story telling to bring the national curriculum alive. He has recently completed a programme for Key Stage 2 on the holocaust. For more information, see www.keystage-company.co.uk.

Mike Levy can be contacted via email at mike.levy@ntlworld.com.

LAWPACK

© 2001 Law Pack Publishing Limited
76-89 Alscot Road
London SE1 3AW

www.lawpack.co.uk
All rights reserved.

ISBN 1 902646 74 6

Contents

Introduction

What this book will do

1. Give you plenty of ideas to get your own effective web site up and running.

2. Give you confidence to ask the right questions when you go to see the specialist web designer (it's like buying a second-hand car, the more you know about the way it works, the better deal you're likely to get with the trader). This book won't make you an expert on web design, but it will help you become much better informed and have a clearer idea of what it is you're trying to do.

3. Give you lots of professional advice. Most chapters will include a special section - 'What the experts think.' This is largely written by our good friends at KiwiWeb who are at the daily chalk face of web building. Sometimes their views may be a little controversial and you may not always agree with them but the internet is nothing if not a community of diverse views.

What the book will not do

1. Give you a general introduction to the internet.

2. Serve as a primer for html code - there are plenty of other books that do this and in any case messing around with code is something you may wish to leave to the experts.

3. Tell you how to set up your own web page. Again, there are plenty of books that can do this for you (provided you have lots of spare time to master layout and code).

Also, if you really want to set up a professional web site - you really only have two alternatives, either to buy the special design software (the market leaders include Microsoft Front Page and Macromedia's Dreamweaver), both of which are excellent but will certainly take you time to master; or to hire the services of a specialised web designer.

Web designers don't come cheap but drawing on the knowledge of a specialist will save time and money in the long run. If your budget is tight however, you could hire a web designer to draw up an outline plan of your proposed web site - rather like going to an architect to have your vision put into a design that can be followed.

This book is for anyone that is considering having a presence on the world wide web. That includes people who have something to sell - products or services, individuals and organisations that have a message to communicate. As you probably know, the internet is a communication tool whose power could barely be guessed at even five years ago. It's not just businesses that are looking to develop an effective web site. These days forward looking schools, clubs, societies, interest groups - the list is endless - are going on the web. Now it's your turn.

Acknowledgements

Thanks must go to the KiwiWeb Design Team who bring their practical knowledge and experience to the book. Here is the team:

Sales & Marketing
Murad Tanjeer (Sales & Marketing)
Email: sales@kiwiweb.co.uk

Design & Development
Francesca Balvert (Front-end Designer)
Email: webdesign@kiwiweb.co.uk

Sue Paterson (Back-end Developer)
Email: webworks@kiwiweb.co.uk

Chris McGrath (Corporate & Creative Writer)
Email: webwords@kiwiweb.co.uk

Susan D Claridge (Corporate & Unique Artworks)
Email: suzydarts@kiwiweb.co.uk

Accounts
Dawn Reed (Company Law)
Email: weblaw@kiwiweb.co.uk

Pete Winstanley (Domains & Hosting)
Email: weburl@kiwiweb.co.uk

Technical & Systems Administrator
Mick Reed (Webmaster)
Email: webmaster@kiwiweb.co.uk

Chapter 1

Why do you need a web site?

Chapter 1

Why do you need a web site?

Summary

· So why have a site?
· What do you want to say?
· Your visitors

This may seem like a very odd question, but it's where you should be starting. Investment in a good web site is not for the fainthearted - it will cost time and money. Also, you need to be sure that the site is really what you and your organisation need. There are plenty of poor reasons why people go for web sites:

- It's expected of us

- We just like to keep ahead of the times

- It will save us a lot of money in marketing

- We don't need it today but we'll put something up there just to show willing

Like puppies, web sites are not just for Christmas or any other specific time of the year. Remember that once you go online, your web site is there for all to see 24/7, 365/365, 5/5 (five continents out of five). Stick up a moribund or empty web site and you are likely to be doing far more harm than good.

So why have a site?

Let's ask the experts:

'Having a web site is a superb opportunity to reach literally thousands, no, millions even, of diverse people at a global level! You know the world is a global village. You know by now that information is the new international currency. Can you really afford to be without using the internet, the up to date tool that everyone's talking about? Is it a flash in the pan, the latest craze or simply the novelty of post-20th century Thatcherite go-getters? Ignore the warning signals that briefly suspend you and replace those warning signs with pound, dollar, yen and DM signs! I mean it must be good! Everyone is doing it, yes? Doing what? Rumour has it you could make a fortune through selling online! This must be how it works! Slap a standard four-page web site up on the internet, sit back for a few weeks, and wait for that filthy lucre to roll in… sounds easy doesn't it?

Well it is and it isn't. Like everything else in life you really do get out what you put in and web-based marketing solutions are no exception. You can place yourself at the cutting edge of the information super highway and surf that wave to increased client orders, confidence, loyalty and repeat business or of course you can stick with the tired old half-pagers in the *Evening News*. But the fact you have bought this book shows that you are interested in finding out what a total web-based solutions package can do for your turnover, profit margins, market exposure and reputation in general.'

KiwiWeb

Consider the 3 Ws:

1. Why? Why do you want a web site?

2. What? What exactly do you want your visitors to do?

3. Who? Who are your visitors?

The three Ws are essentially www.(dot!) A web site can be one of two things. It's up to you to decide. You can have a half-hearted stab and leave it hanging out there to rot, year after year, gathering the cyber equivalent of moth balls while secretly yearning for those halcyon days of the *Evening News* half-pagers. Or you could approach it with the same level of commitment you approach your client base or indeed any other aspect of your business or interest. After all, if you can't be bothered to take your message seriously and get it out there where people can benefit from the products and services you have to offer, then why should anyone give a damn what you have to say? The bottom line in today's market place is that the guy that doesn't take care of business is pretty soon out of business.

Remember - a web site is not there for your benefit. It is there to help your visitors. So there are two basic questions:

1. What is it that you want to say to your visitors to the site?

2. Who are your likely visitors?

Let's look at each in turn.

What do you want to say?

It is very surprising that many people and organisations are prepared to spend time and money setting up an expensive web site, without having first thought about its function. What is it there for? What result do I expect to get from this web site? The reason for this careless approach is that the internet can be very alluring: it is easy to think that just by having a web site, all kinds of benefits will fall into your lap - more customers, a bigger market share, more street cred, fame and fortune.

It's true that the internet is an incredibly powerful medium of communications but it is about communications, and that means making sure you know what your message is supposed to be!

'We spent thousands on a company web site that did little more than tell the world we were here. The trouble is that our customers - even potential customers - knew we were here already. That's not what we should have been telling them. Looking back we should have made more of the really key message about a change in the way we managed the company.'

MD of a small company.

Before you begin thinking about your web site, spend a little time on your key messages. Remember the internet is a communications tool. So, what do you want to communicate?

1. Information about your company organisation (that can't perhaps be easily found elsewhere). This could include:

    - the latest news on your product or service range;

    - up to the minute price list;

    - new services coming on stream;

    - technical support documents (or frequently asked questions about your products or services);

    - your contact details including name, address, telephone, fax and the all important email links so that visitors can get straight to the person they need in your organisation.

    You may also want to include feedback forms to ask customers or users what they think of your product or service. This is where the internet really scores - giving you a direct link to your customers, users or interest group.

    This is just a small sample of the kinds of information you may wish to communicate via the web - you will learn more as you work through this book.

2. Offer the world an image of you and your organisation. Image is everything these days and the internet is incredibly powerful in supporting that. You can create memorable logos, an in-house colour scheme, a strong brand image; you can use pictures, graphics, animations, video, audio or sound clips (even a statement from the boss but go easy on that idea - internet attention span is notoriously short). In a multi-media age, you are limited only by your imagination (OK and maybe budget too).

As you will see in the next chapter, there is so much to be learnt from looking at other people's web sites.

Your visitors

You shouldn't start to think about your web site until you have a clear idea or profile of your likely visitors to the site.

Know your visitors

- What are visitors thinking when they come to your site? The more you can get into the head of the visitor, the closer your web site will be to meet their needs. What are they asking themselves when they visit your site?

- Does the domain name reflect the purpose of the site? It is reassuring for visitors to go to a site whose name clearly describes the functions of the site. For instance, if you were looking for a site that offered to make trophies and medals, how would you feel if it were called zanyDali.com? Or something really obscure such as whizz-Ben-1037.net? Far better to give it a name that includes trophies or medals - or at least suggests these products.

- Did the page (or pages) load up quickly enough? Remember that in the online world people are fidgety and will move on unless they see what they want to see in under ten seconds.

- Was the site simple to navigate? In other words, how easy is it to get from page to page or link to link on your site? Some sites that are poorly planned make it very difficult for the user to find the pages they want. Even with a good site map it can be difficult to find your way around a badly planned web site. The trouble

---

Domain names - what the experts think

If your company identity and brand are important to you (and we are assuming that it is) decide on a short punchy quirky name. So what do we look for when choosing a domain name? Is your domain name relevant to your site content? It doesn't need to be. Take the huge multi-national companies, for example, IBM and HP - what do these have to do with hardware? The point here is you should choose a domain name that matches (or fits) your company identity and keep it short and snappy! Users suffer from memory relapse and long domain names just do not stick! So given your most recently acquired memory lapse - let's recap. Use: 1. a name that is easy to remember; 2. easy to spell; and 3. easy to pronounce! The world wide web is complex enough without adding another complexity! Keep it simple!

You should also be aware that if you buy a separate package or an add-on to an existing package through a professional that they are less likely to be prepared to accept .org or .net extensions. These are secondary extensions to .com or .co.uk and thought of as amateurish or less used in a professional context. Extensions at one time used to mean something before the web went wild and sold names to less than creditable companies!

---

is that you may know your pages too well - always try the site out with a friendly observer - someone whom you can trust to be honest and critical.

- Was the site interesting, informative and relevant? Did it speak to me? Did it use the language that I feel comfortable with? Did it make me feel secure that I was in a trustworthy environment?

- Was I asked to give lots of personal information without knowing why? This can be a huge turn-off for visitors to a site - being asked for name, address, phone number and so on without good reason. They may well ask: 'What are they going to do with all this information? Why are they being so nosy? Am I going to be put on a junk mail list?' Be very careful about asking for personal information.

- Is there enough of interest in the site to make me want to come back for more?

Putting up a web site is no different from any other kind of communication or marketing strategy. You need to have a clear picture of the user, visitor, client, customer or member.

The home page of a web site is its window to the world. It's the page that most visitors will arrive at when they decide to come and have a look at your web site. This is where the decision to stay or go is often made, but it's surprising how untempting the home page can be. It's the place where many would-be designers and interested amateurs mistakenly like to stick all their flashy animations or screen-size illustrations. This erroneous thinking often comes from the world of print where a striking front cover is needed, but a home page is not a front cover, it is more a welcoming door to the rest of the building. So what are the key features of a good home page?

It offers a warm welcome and does this through a careful use of colour and image placement. The text and images on a home page should clearly tell the visitor where they are, what the site will offer, and doesn't require too much scrolling up and down. That means that all the key functions of the home page are seen on-screen in one visual bite. Try to avoid a home page that is too crowded with text, graphics, animations, sound files or a myriad of links. In other words, a home page should be clear, clean and very easy to read.

One of the most common problems of the home page is that authors try to put everything on it (for fear of losing a visitor). The danger of this is that all the key messages and vital nuggets of information may be at the very bottom of a long home page requiring lots of tiresome scrolling. Remember that the home page is just part of your web site - it is the gateway through which your visitors can travel to the rest of the site. That means that you should plan your home page along with all the other pages.

Try to avoid the common mistake of designing a home page first and then thinking about the rest of the site later. In this way the home page and the sub pages will be much more closely integrated. Have a look at some of your favourite web sites and study the home page carefully. What can you learn from it? Does it follow the golden rule of 'K i s s' ('Keep it simple, stupid!'), and what have they done to make the design and colour scheme welcoming?

One of the basic design principles in any walk of life is consistency. There should be a consistent theme running through the work helping to unify the set of disparate ideas. In terms of a web site with many pages, the design should provide the visitor with a sense that he or she is moving around the same environment no matter how many pages are being visited. The simple way to insure consistency is to create a design theme that runs throughout the site. That means that each page (and remember there may be hundreds) recalls in the visitor's mind all the other pages on the site. It's not just about consistency of colour - in fact it would be a dull web site that offered the same colour on every page. Nor is it about consistency of layout - it's an even duller web site that has the same number of columns, frames, headings, illustrations, etc.

Consistency of design means that there are one or more elements that pull everything in the same direction. It could be, for instance, that each page referring to a product or service has a certain colour scheme and each page that refers to information or contact details has a different colour scheme. Consistency of design is something that is best left to the experts (or at least those with some experience), but we will be looking at some of the principles of design later in the book. One of the things that you should certainly be consistent about is clarity. Remember that most sites communicate their key messages by text. Text on a screen is often much harder to read than text in a book. This is especially true if the designer has used lots of background graphics or a background colour on which the text cannot be read clearly (I have seen one site that used white text against a grey background - that might look OK on a T-shirt but certainly not on a computer screen where it was virtually invisible).

Identifying your visitors

Though this may seem a bit simplistic, your visitors could be placed into 3 or 4 neat categories (at least for the sake of initial analysis):

1. **People who know about you** and are ready to find out more. These are the determined visitors who may have been before, maybe existing customers,

people who know you by reputation, visitors to other sites who have been directed to yours, people who have subscribed to your club, membership list, invitation and so on.

2. **Free and easy surfers.** Regular users of the internet who spend perhaps hours a week surfing the net, looking for sites of interest to them. These surfers are still a distinct minority (probably less than ten per cent of the internet population). They're like gadflies flitting from one site to another. They may spend very little time on your site, perhaps only seconds. So if these are the people you want, you're going to have to grab their attention quickly! The good news about these surfers is that once they are hooked, they are likely to come back, so it's up to you to provide decent bait.

3. **Occasional dippers.** These are people who like the internet but only spend a short time every week online. That's because they may have little time or can only access the net at weekends (or if they are parents of teenage children, they may get little opportunity to use the computer). This group is potentially very interesting. Because time is short they want to use their online experience in the most effective way. If a dipper comes your way, he or she is there for a purpose. If you have something to sell or something to say, do it quickly, crisply and simply.

4. **Good time guys.** These are people who mainly use the net for fun. They go on line to play games, download music, scour the entertainment pages, have a flutter, enjoy some gossip, read about the stars. Your site will have to be fun, entertaining and fulfilling in a way that other sites are not. Competition will be great and you will need a real USP - Unique Selling Point to attract and keep visitors.

Tip

Spend some time and money finding out who your likely visitors are and why they might want to come to your site. Build up a profile of them in terms of:

- which type of visitor - people you know, surfers, good time guys etc.;

- age and gender profile;

- income and spending habits;

- interests and hobbies;

- other sites they like to visit;

- how long they spend online each day or week;

- whether or not they are used to spending money online;

- what security or guarantees they need to feel secure about buying anything from you (and I use 'buying' in the broadest sense - not necessarily an exchange of money)?

What the experts think

So now you know why you want a site and should already have some clear ideas how to make it a really successful one. You want to reach new market niches, you want to make it easier for your target audience to find you and, of course, you want to take a leap into the future where staying ahead of the game is the difference between winning and losing. What exactly do you want your visitors to do? Well you know the answer to that one! The beauty of this medium is you decide! You want to give your visitors an overview of your national retail outlets? No problem! You want to have the facilities for real-time transaction processing i.e. buying online? Again, no problem! Or maybe you want a hint of mystique! Maybe you provide a unique and specialist service that a select few pay top dollar for the privilege of accessing while you can give as much or as little information as you want. You are totally in charge. You see the correct web-based solutions package should be just that - a complete solution. Not just a sexier mode of advertising, not just a company biography, not even a funky way of presenting a more hi-tech, glitzy image but all of these things and much more!

Chapter 2

Aim for the highest

Chapter 2

Aim for the highest

Summary

· Where do you begin?
· Strengths and weaknesses of web sites
· Learning from other web sites
· Web site award winners and losers

So, where do you begin? The best place to find good web design is probably sitting right in front of you, that's if you're working at a computer and you have access to the internet. There are literally millions of web sites out there - many are pretty poor, but you will find some excellent ones. So why reinvent the wheel? Just spend a morning (or a couple of evenings) surfing the net and looking for good examples of top quality web sites. You can learn so much from close study of a good, well designed, carefully constructed web site. That's not to say that you have to copy other web sites - every business, every voluntary organisation, every individual is different. But you can pick up a lot of very useful design tips by looking at existing sites.

So what should you be looking for? And where do you begin? One place to start might be to look at web sites that offer something very similar to you. It is advisable to scan at least 15 to 20 sites that are roughly in your sector. But you should also spent time looking at web sites that are completely outside of your area of interest. After all, this is what thinking laterally is all about. You may, for instance, have a small business selling ladies' fashions and you could learn something from web sites that offer online ticket booking and travel information.

'I got some really good ideas from looking at US web sites offering gambling or catering equipment. Although I'm not in that field, there were some really innovative thoughts that came to me as a result of studying these sites.'

A used car dealer.

When you are looking at other web sites, try to put on your most critical hat. You will learn a lot by studying the site's strengths and weaknesses.

Here are some useful guidelines:

A. **Loading time.** How long does it take for the site to load up? In the world of electronic marketplace, people are incredibly impatient. There are so many other sites to visit, why waste your life waiting for some jazzy bit of graphic to load up? If the site does take a long time to load, look for reasons. Has it got too many fancy bits of animation? Is the page overcrowded? If you have to wait for more than five seconds for the page to load, you can give it the thumbs down!

Some sites load up quickly but have a very long opening page - you might have to scroll down a long way to get to the bit you really need (such as a contact name or link into another page). If you can't get to the bit you really need quickly and efficiently, then the site has failed.

However, if you come to a site that pops up in a trice and has all the links you are looking for without too much scrolling - then this is the one to learn from. Make a note of the web site's address and come back to it later.

B. **How does it look?** Design, of course, comes down to personal taste, but most of us know a turkey when we see one. If the page offends your eye by being too garish, too dull, too messy or too jumbled, then you can thank the web designer of this page for showing you how it should not be done.

C. **Who is the site aimed at and does it succeed?** If, for instance, the site gives advice on funeral arrangements, does it do so tastefully or does it play a stupid jingle as you load up? (Perhaps a rock version of the death march?)

It is always worth asking what the site is aiming to do - and is it succeeding? For instance, if the aim is to suggest a high quality service, does the site design reflect this message? This is down to a whole range of factors: colour scheme, page arrangements, copy (written style), illustrations, links to other web sites, advertising and so on.

If the site is aimed at children, is the design eye-catching, appropriate in tone, set at the right level of language, not too patronising, easy to navigate, completely up to date (kids are always on the cutting edge when it comes to computers).

D. **Browser compatibility.** One of the most common pitfalls in web design is that asides that look good in one browser such as Netscape Navigator may look awful in another such as Internet Explorer. The way to tell is easy: checkout the site in both browsers (and any others visitors to your site may use).

We will be looking in more detail at many of these issues in future chapters, but you should start becoming a web site critic from today!

Learning from successful web sites could be the best move you make, but which ones should you look at from so many? One way to narrow down your range of best practice options is to look at the various web site awards presented each year by the Net Community's good and great. The most prestigious web design gong in the UK is probably the annual Yell Awards (held each October). This is open to all comers from the biggest banks to the smallest community sites. The awards are placed in separate categories such as Best Commercial Site or Best Education Site. As an example, the Best Charity Site for 2001 was RSPCA Online (www.rspca.co.uk). The judges at Yell were impressed by the way the site:

- communicated its message;

- made imaginative use of add-ons such as 'cyber pets' and news sections.

The designers of the site also commented that 'Although we have limited funds, we hope to demonstrate that...there is no reason for a charity not to have a well-constructed and professional web site.'

The Yell Site of the Year in 2001 was neither a big company, nor a national charity but a small local community site. Caithness Community (www.caithness.org) certainly was able to punch above its weight. It was created in 1999 by a father and son team along with a few volunteers. Why did it win? According to the Yell Award, 'The site manages to combine the freshness of grass-roots activism with a high degree of professionalism.' They also point to the site's potential audience, 'Originally intended just for people in the UK's most northerly county, it quickly outgrew this role, with the web site's exhaustive content and commerce attracting a global audience.'

Emphasising that small can indeed be beautiful, the winner of the Yell Commerce Site Award was Crocus (www.crocus.co.uk), a gardening site that the judges described as 'really fantastic' and 'really clever.' Praise was given for its attention to detail, such as email advice on how to look after the plant you have just purchased from the site. They also liked the balance of ecommerce and gardening advice, positioning itself not just as a retailer but also a sector expert.

Another industry award for good web design is given by Eye-Dentity - actually a design company based in England (www.eye-dentity.net).

Their advice on what judges are looking for in granting an award to a web site is worth noting:

'Appearances are not everything. Your web site may look wonderful, but how well does it function behind the scenes? Are you conveying your message effectively? Are you using that Java applet just because you can, or does it actually serve a purpose?'

EYE-DENTITY award points on each of the following criteria:

- **Functionality:** Browser compatibility, loading speed, ease of navigation, working databases, interactive areas and so on.

- **Layout and aesthetics:** Effective use of tables and/or frames, harmonious use of colours, appropriate typography.

- **Consistency:** Fonts and backgrounds should be consistent on each page. There should be no broken links or images.

- **Content and copy:** Content should be informative, interesting and well written. Make us want to come back! There should be no grammatical or spelling errors.

- **Technology:** Effective (not gratuitous) use of technologies such as Flash, DHTML, Java, PHP, CGI, ASP, Shockwave and so on.

They urge potential award winners not to include these technologies '..just because you can. Include them because they enhance your site. If they don't, leave them out.'

It is also useful to look at Eye-Dentity's slightly tongue-in-cheek advice on how NOT to win awards:

- Put a 500kb graphic of your pet poodle on your home page, and then expect people to sit there and wait for it to load.

- Stick as many animations, marquees and flying pop up windows on your site as you can. If possible put most of these on your home page, to keep the poodle company.

- Change fonts, font sizes and font colours at every available opportunity. Underline some of it as well, so that people mistake ordinary text for links. Finally, use the most garish background that you can find (animated if possible) so that nobody can read your text anyway.

- Make sure that you have really long pages (yes, even longer than this one) with all the text sitting squarely in the middle. Also remember that space is there to be filled. Every last inch of it.

- Use as much web technology as possible and force your visitors to download lots of plug-ins before they can enter your site. Also use some big Java applets, especially those nice lake ones that take an eternity to load.

- Find some really badly arranged MIDI files and embed them into every single page. Even better, do this without giving your visitors any way of turning them off.

- Make sure that most of your links don't work. While you're at it, also ensure that a few of your images are broken. The odd 404-error message wouldn't go amiss either.

- Design your site for resolutions of 1280x1024 pixels or above. So what if most of your audience can't see it? They'll just have to scroll horizontally.

- On the same subject, design everything for your favourite browser. If it doesn't work in another one, that's too bad. People will just have to download the one YOU use.

- Don't bother making your own web graphics. Just 'borrow' some and claim them as your own. Feel free to resize, recolour, and otherwise massacre them to your heart's content. After all, the original creator will never find out you've used their work, will they? (Note: In this case, they did. We made sure of it).

Source: www.eye-dentity.net.

Eye-Dentity also provides useful pointers to what might lose points in a judgement of a web site:

Download time:

Your site should download within a reasonable time. A wait of more than three minutes for your home page to download over a 56k connection will mean that we will leave your site without viewing it further.

Originality and visual appeal:

Your web site should be unique - be creative! It should be visually appealing, with no broken internal links or images. Advertising banners should be kept to a minimum. Pop-up windows are acceptable if they are an integral part of your site's design.

Navigation:

Your site must be easy to navigate - we should be able to reach any of your pages with no more than three mouse clicks. If your navigation relies on technologies such as Flash or Java, you must ensure that people without those technologies can still find their way around your site with no problems.

Browser compatibility:

Your site should function well in recent versions of both Internet Explorer and Netscape. We will take into account certain discrepancies when using Netscape 6 as many people (ourselves included) are still in the process of amending their code to make their scripts fully functional for this browser. Your site should be viewable at screen resolutions of 800x600 or higher without the need for horizontal scrolling.

Advanced web technologies:

We actively encourage the effective use of advanced web technologies, providing that they don't crash our browsers. Should this happen, you can be certain that your site will not win an award.

Background music:

Forcing people to listen to a terrible MIDI rendition of 'Stairway to Heaven' may not be everyone's idea of site enhancement. If you use music on your site, please give people the option of turning it off!

Spelling, grammar and consistency:

Spelling mistakes and grammatical errors will adversely affect our final decision. Lack of consistency (fonts, font sizes, backgrounds and so on) will also go against you.

Privacy policies:

If your site requires visitors to provide any personal information (such as email addresses or credit card details for example) you must provide an easily accessible privacy policy that states exactly what any collected data is used for.

Awards pages and link backs:

You must have a separate awards page, and this must be clearly accessible from your home page. After all, what is the point of applying for awards if your have no intention of displaying them?

Source www.eye-dentity.net.

Another well-respected award based in the UK is the Médaille d'Or Awards. According to their judges, when they look at a web site they ask:

'Does it instantly impress and does it seem to convey an enthusiasm for its subject? But we also ask ourselves whether the site is both usable and useful. Are download times reasonable? Is the site kept reasonably up to date? Is navigation straightforward and intuitive? Does the content make the site worth exploring? Is it attractive? Is it fun?'

It's an important last point - web sites should be attractive and (where appropriate) fun to visit. Keep remembering: It is a communications tool first and foremost!

The Médaille d'Or Awards judges also provide some invaluable advice for would-be site designers. These come as a series of searching questions:

- Does that banner ad across the top of your main page really add to the carefully worked atmosphere you are striving for? (And how can you tell when you can't control its content?)

- How do you expect your visitors to react to multiple banner ads or, still worse, flying window ads?

- How many splash screens do you expect your visitors to plough through before they get to the substance of your site? Why do you need one at all? How long do you expect them to wait for your animation to load?

- And when they get there, how many different fonts; how many flashing graphics; how many large files; and how many discordant midi themes or colour combinations do you think they will stand before they go somewhere more comfortable?

- Have you considered what your site would look like on a different-sized screen to the one you normally use? Does your background image repeat itself on a wider screen? And what does it look like on a different browser? Does it even work on a different browser?

What they are urging here is that you should always think about the web site from the viewpoint of the visitor surfing into it for the first time.

They also provide a good set of ten reasons why your site might fail their scrutiny:

10 best ways to avoid winning The Médaille d'Or:

1.   Design your site for one browser only, and insist your visitors use it.

2.   Force your visitors to sit through a high bandwidth Flash intro to your site without any way of skipping it. (After all, how often do you watch the full motion intro to your favourite computer game?)

3.   Lock your visitors into your site by disabling the 'Back' button.

4. Design in small red text on black or livid blue. Add in a starry background, twinkling if possible. Enhance the design further with lots of slow loading animated .gif files. Flickering torches are especially effective.

5. Expect your visitors to wait for your wonderful 300kb intro graphic to download.

6. Go for a design philosophy based on big text, centre justified, splurged down the length of a long page and broken up with a bunch of neat horizontal lines.

7. Ask visitors to tell you their name when they arrive at your site and put up a farewell window asking them to remember to sign your visitors' book when they leave.

8. Give visitors more banner ads than content to look at; clutter up their system with flying screens; and expect them to wait while your favourite music file downloads for their entertainment.

9. Ensure you have placed as much Flash animation and as many splash screens as possible between your visitors and your content.

10. Have a <BLINK> command anywhere on your site.

Source www.arachnid.co.uk/index.html.

Chapter 3

DIY or hire a professional?

Chapter 3

DIY or hire a professional?

Summary

· How to choose a good web professional
· What about DIY?

Whatever reasons you have for building a site, they all have one thing in common, to convey information to millions of users or web surfers on a global scale. So now you can see that the benefit of a complete web-based solutions package is multi-faceted. All those millions can be reached in a cyber second in a way that no other medium can even come close to matching. Have you even thought for a second about how ridiculously easy breaking foreign markets and client bases could be by harnessing the power of web-based technology? Exciting isn't it! Well we've got news for you: We haven't even started yet! Hang on for the ride - it just gets better!

The 3 W's are related to your competencies in correctly identifying the viability of your organisation's requirements, given market research and analysis. The big question is: Do you hire a professional web builder or go for a DIY approach?

Hiring a professional web builder does cost. However, if you feel you're about to embark on a time consuming journey into unknown territory, then leave it to a professional. A good and competent professional, fluent in IT practices, would benefit you.

How to choose a good web professional

It's not easy - there are so many around and there are no industry kite mark standards to follow. The best advice is to go on reputation and go armed with the right set of questions. Your Yellow Pages will be bursting with web professionals (unless you live in a very remote spot but even these days there are web wizards hiding out in the most isolated glens).

A good web professional should offer you initial consultation that is either free or very low cost. He or she will (or should) try to establish a thorough analysis of your business or organisation's requirements, together with a unique and creative identity. An organisation can build and develop on this foundation by training an employee in the duties of a webmaster, given the appropriate web training over time. The crucial rule, obvious though it may seem, is the first essential element of any successful venture, basically, 'First Impressions Count.' And within the New Media industry, should you annoy your users with crude first impressions? To ask the question is to answer it!

A competent and reputable professional should offer you a 'total web-based solutions package,' which, among many other things (some of which we will be looking at later on) will include addressing the 3 W's in relation to your specific requirements. This may be a long and involved process, but is an essential one prior to the conceptual design and development stage of the site. In the wonderful world of the web, the old maxim is true - do not run before you can walk!

Should you use a friend, colleague or local IT-savvy teenager? It is amazing how many web sites are created by 'gifted amateurs,' lured by the promise of 'it's all in the box' web-building software. That's not to say you can't make a very good-looking site using this software but it's only a tool. Buying an easel and paintbrushes does not make a Michelangelo.

Getting an amateur to build a web site is probably asking for trouble. In his hurry to complete a given project, he will not take into account the majority of the underlying factors that are linked to a successful venture. The project will have little or no structure and little thought as to what it is the site ought to do. He might ask you what a strategic marketing plan is? If he does, you're in trouble! It shows that the would-be designer has little knowledge or experience of the marketing potential of the world wide web.

The content of his site might very well be a conglomeration of 'graphics, garbage and irrelevant garble.' He will probably show you how clever he is in utilising rich-media content in Flash. I wonder where he downloaded his movies? Be wary of those who might promise you a full interactive site and then leave you to it.

And at that crucial stage when you plan to update, the would-be designer is nowhere to be found. His number's changed in that time or he has decided to return to university to complete his final year in Computer Science, having taken a year out 'to chill.' What good is 'chilling' to you?

What the experts think

Watch out for graphics junkies. Graphics, funky though they are, just do not adhere to web standards. The sizes are huge and he insists on transferring these graphics onto your web page, regardless of whether you like it or not. Should you be brave enough to suggest exactly what it is you want, beware of the sniggers and back chat and your typical response of 'well okay' until you find your site designed the way he wanted it! Having paid a percentage upfront, or even the full amount given the enormous discount, you now feel disconcerted, irritable and really annoyed. Now ask yourself what you should do now? Totally fed up with his bad attitude, lack of consideration and typical one liners like: 'Yeah man…it's great! My friends like it,' you decide that web culture is but a farce. But maybe you've just had a bad experience and made the wrong decision. Alternatively, you may have been lucky and are at present disdainfully scanning this portion of the book. For your sake, I do hope you're one of the lucky ones.

Eventually after a long period of grudgingly agreeing to yet another extension date until the completion of your site, it is now up and running. Or so you think! Having checked your site you find a number of so-called implemented web technologies are just not working and you are finding those fatal errors! Patience is wearing thin and temper tantrums are many! And furthermore, where the hell is he?

It might be a cheaper alternative, and within your budgetary constraints, but ask yourself this - will it damage my offline reputation? Four pages of a professional put together standard site (that of which includes 1. an introductory home page; 2. a biography on page 3. Further information pertaining to your company and/or services; 4. a contact page) together with a decent web hosting package is worth 10,000 pages more than this numb nut will put together for you! There are other alternatives and/or web technology add-ons as you well know, but initially keep it simple. Consider this before you consider 'the kid next door.'

What about DIY?

This is fine, but unless you have real design talents, your web site will always look amateurish. That is not to say you don't have a say. You, and not the designer, know where the priorities lie. You are in touch with your niche market.

A really common mistake for amateurs to make is to forget about image optimisation - making sure that the delicate balance between size and resolution is maintained. All too often DIY attempts at using site creation software packages (which cost up to £1,000) end in slow downloads, error messages and pages that look like a template (that's where they probably came from).

What the experts think

Months ahead the DIY web builder will wonder why that wonderful web tool 'stats tracker' only reads two hits a day. Studiously reading the most recent articles pertaining to the 'Top 10 web promotional strategies' he can be found downloading trial versions of software packages - those that sincerely guarantee 'success with ease and a few clicks away!' These packages supposedly take the hard graft out of tedious work. Strange as it may seem this creature can be found furiously submitting, and time and time again, his URL to every possible search engine the world wide web has ever known.

After a few months, auto-response emails from unknown search engines confirm his URL submission, thanking him personally (and thanking him personally...and thanking him personally!) before mysteriously disappearing. Did he ever wonder why his mailbox was filled with an overwhelming amount of junk mail and porn?

And so his site is tucked away with the many thousand sites that blend and finally dissolve into this cyber spider world of search engine automation. Never to be seen or heard of again! Not even the most competent of web surfers could possibly hope to find it. But he has done what he can! Surely? And again old misconceptions of web technologies and their uselessness rear their ugly head and bobble angrily to the surface. That the evolving web technology is nothing but a farce! That it doesn't work! Remember the web is an effective tool and medium but there is a need to utilise and implement it correctly.

However, through attaining the appropriate knowledge there is a chance (and a slim one at that) that the DIY masochist could successfully design and develop his own site. Amongst the errors of his proposed project design and development, the DIY masochist has only one thought in mind and that is to succeed. Given his hope to succeed he will do so eventually. If not online it will be offline. After all his business pays for his leisure time and those material goodies we all hope to acquire...one day. Let's hope though that the rapidly evolving internet technologies do not leave this fumbling masochist behind!

You may have gathered by now that we are not in favour of DIY or 'Phone a friend' methods of web building. If your budget is very tight and your expectations low, then by all means consider learning a site development package but otherwise, your money will be far better spent with a professional designer. In fact, it's far better to buy a day or two of their time and go for cheap web design software (some are shareware and very cheap). You can even build a perfectly usable web site using Netscape Navigator. Word processing packages such as Microsoft Word also have basic but serviceable web templates.

Don't forget, that even if you employ a professional web designer, you need to go armed with a clear idea of what you need. That includes all the stuff we've been talking about so far (aim of the site, visitors etc.) and some clear strategy for choosing a name, preferred hosting company and marketing strategy. Plus you should work out what you want to say on the site and that might mean writing the text pages. Don't leave that to the professionals unless you know and really trust them - and they know you.

Chapter 4

Choosing a hosting company

Chapter 4

Choosing a hosting company

Summary

· What to look for in choosing an ISP

Registering a domain name is easy but you have to do it online. There are dozens, if not hundreds, of ISPs urging you to register with them and you may be tempted by ads that offer registration for 2p per month or some such ridiculously small amount. Beware of these - such offers are usually masterpieces of small print where all kinds of hidden costs have to be added on such as tax, two-year sign-ups and 'one off' charges. Many sites that offer low cost registration will insist that you carry one of their advertising banners. This can mean that every time someone clicks on to your site, your ISP's banner (or someone else they have done deals with) barges into view - often obscuring your home page message. So the advice is to pay a bit more to have a name properly registered without freebies, special offers or low cost 'once-in-a-lifetime' deals.

Most, if not all, registry companies will offer to host your site - in other words, they are ISPs.

How do you find the ISP to suit your needs? One way is to get advice from your professional web designer. But beware, there may be vested interests at play. It's worth doing some investigation of your own. There are plenty of monthly magazines, such as *Internet Magazine*, which regularly rank and compare ISPs. You could decide to choose an ISP based in the USA - but if you expect most of your visitors to come from the UK, it probably makes more sense to choose a host based here - as pages may load up more quickly. There are several sites that provide an independent comparison of ISPs. One of the best is www.findahost.com. This site will allow you to compare thousands of host companies and you can choose which features you wish to have included. You may wish, for instance, to have 24-hour toll-free telephone support (very useful if you're running the site yourself - some ISPs charge as much as £1 per minute for support and a query can easily take ten minutes to resolve).

What to look for in choosing an ISP

Make sure they offer you enough space on their server, but how much is enough? That depends on the potential size of your site. 20 megabytes of disk space is plenty for most small organisations and you can always pay more to buy additional space later.

Make sure they support the use of CGI scripts. What are CGI scripts? They are useful little applications that add all kinds of features to your web site:

- **Email forms** - a brilliant way of getting feedback from your visitors, clients or members. The form may say, for instance, 'I am interested in finding out more about your organisation. My name is. My email address is.' You can also add a space for your visitors' comments or questions.

- **Search feature** - this allows your visitors to search your site for specific information. It's a very professional addition and you should make sure that your ISP supports this CGI script.

- **Guest book** - another way to get great feedback from your visitors who can sign in, give their comments, ask questions, share information and so on.

- **Searchable database** - this allows visitors to access information held on one or more databases. This could include: What's on in the area, properties for sale, best price in the local market, etc.

- **Hit counters** - they keep track of the number of hits to your site (more specifically to a web page). If you're going to use them, place a hit counter on the home page - it's just there as a general guide and not a substitute for proper monitoring of site activity. This should be done by using specialist software called 'log analysis tools.'

- **Chat rooms** - great if you want to build a sense of community. They provide visitors with a space in which to type messages to each other. This may be useful if you want to build a sense of camaraderie between your visitors or establish an online community of members or users.

There are many more CGI scripts including calendars, sitemaps, clocks and even games and interactive story boards (where visitors can add their contributions to an ongoing piece of text like a story). When you sign up with an ISP, check which CGI scripts they support on their server.

What the experts think

Which web hosting company?

The biggest problem you will face is which web hosting company to look for. This is a make or break issue which will reflect on your business as a whole, and for a long time to come. Not just in terms of finance, although obviously this is crucial, but also in terms of the damage a wrong choice can do to your image and consequently your business. Can a company survive constant downtime? A slow connection? It is common knowledge (through merely surfing the web) that if a site is unattainable or it takes too long to load your users will venture onto the next site and take a peek there instead. A potential client lost, a possible order gone to the competition, maybe a lifetime relationship with a blue chip layer squandered because of a bad decision on choice of hosting company. What a shame that would be... The cyber equivalent of the 'kiss of death even! And that is no exaggeration.

A final word here. There seems to be a strange acceptance among all aspects of computing but particularly online functions, that poor performance, mysterious glitches and inexplicable happenings reminiscent of the strange shenanigans more commonly associated with the twilight zone are 'just the way it is.' There is almost a reverential fear to criticising or attempting to demand better from the great God of computing. Well, let me tell you that this is rubbish! The world, like it or not, is a market place and in a market place you not only get what you pay for but you also deserve what you pay for!

> ### Tip
>
> Take your time, pick and choose, and maybe even try a few out on a trial basis. In any event, this is a key decision you will have to make and when your hard earned cash is flowing in this direction you need a provider that can and does deliver consistently. Week in week out, year in year out.

Receiving poor service and performance from your web hosting company? Kick up a fuss and move on if they don't shape up presto! There are plenty of eager beavers out there just dying to have your business, and, of course, if they won't take care of your business then they are costing you business.

So when you are choosing a web hosting company, think very carefully. What is it you are looking for? Is it reliability or the best deal? Of course, everybody seems to be looking for the best deal these days, at least as far as 'best' is equated with 'cheapest.' If they were familiar with the potential woes of a bad-hosting company, would they be that quick? No one is saying you have to pay through the nose but here as in everything else we have previously looked at, you do get what you pay for.

A good professional will offer this to you as an additional package or possibly as part of a total web-based solutions package. A professional will take over the boring, time consuming, and therefore by definition, the costly, housekeeping duties most commonly associated with managing the web site. These housekeeping duties are tedious, so beware, and so are technical support, site administration and security.

These, of course, are examples only and are by no stretch of the imagination the whole picture. A 'site management package' is, of course, an extra cost! Another extra cost? I hear you wail! Well just think for a moment of the migraines just lurking in wait to strike you down if suddenly you needed support, to change site content, to immediately deal with security alerts! Relegating to a professional is clearly the most sensible and, in the long run, the most cost effective way of managing your site. However, consider the following for your own peace of mind:

1. **Technical support**

Can the hosting company you have decided upon offer your site adequate support? Take into consideration the length of time a server can be down for. Hosting companies' abilities will impact upon your business. You obviously want this impact to be of the positive rather than the negative variety.

2. **Contention**

It is imperative for you to know at least roughly what a web hosting company's contention is, so find out how many other sites share your server. The more people that connect to that hosting company the slower it is. The slower it is, the bigger risk of irate and impatient users moving on to someone else's site.

3. **Bandwidth**

The hosting company you have selected needs to be able to handle a great number of hits and still ensure you get a reasonable user connection. This is a concern if the other sites on the server are flooded with visitors and those hoping to visit your web site may not be able to get through. Check the policy. If your site increases in popularity there may be an extortionate fee.

4. **Site administration**

Check your chosen hosting company's 'user-friendliness.' How secure and user-friendly is the software you'll be using? Remember those tedious housekeeping duties?

And additionally, remember to update pages, manage files, collect orders and retrieve forms, should you decide against a professional and want to do it yourself.

5.   Security and privacy

What security features do the web hosting company offer or support? Can they protect your data from the cyber criminals? They certainly should if they have the gall to take your money for the privilege! Furthermore, how well would they do this? Any idea? Here's a tip: Ensure that you don't connect to the internet through your web hosting company. Most web hosting companies are Internet Service Providers (ISPs) and most ISPs are web-hosting companies. Do not host your site with your ISP. Keep the two separate!

Beware of free hosting companies. They make their money by selling your details on. Try to avoid them at all costs. Have you ever wondered how you managed to accumulate so much junk mail and why it gets to you physically through your door? Well now you know.

Chapter 5

Content rules

Chapter 5

Content rules

Summary

· Important elements in the content of your site
· Brainstorm your content ideas
· Email links
· Graphics

So you've chosen your domain name and have a pretty good idea about hosting companies. You also know something about your visitors - their needs, likes and dislikes. Now it's time to start planning the content of the site.

Why should anyone visit your site? You can have all the fancy graphics in the world - brilliant colours, clever animations, special effects - none of it makes any difference unless the content of your site is interesting, informative, essential, entertaining, up to date, targeted and reliable. Maybe we should have said at the beginning of this book - unless you have something really useful to say, don't bother with the time and expense of a good web site.

Important elements in the content of your site

Where so many sites go wrong is that they don't take enough account of what visitors might need. The golden rule is to put yourself in the shoes of your visitors. What do they need to know?

Your organisation's name

You need a clear description right from the start of who you are and what you're offering. It's amazing how many highly designed sites fail to tell you what the organisation does. I can think of one very well-known company whose site never tells you what they do.

How to contact you - include all telephone, fax, email, snail mail, telex and pigeon courier details. If there are different departments to contact, don't forget the contact details of each. And make it easy for the visitor to navigate to your contact details. That means making it part of your navigation button bar in the home page.

When they can contact you - and don't forget to take into account different time zones. Put your time into GMT if necessary.

Provide a list or outline of your products, services, requirements and objectives. If you're selling something, you're likely to provide a list of your services or products - perhaps photographs, descriptions, current prices, technical details, reviews or customer quotes, delivery times, extra costs such as tax, delivery, packaging, customisation, upgrades and so on.

Providing visitors with support

You may wish to provide details of how people can get support for the products or services your offer. This may include telephone or email support, documentation, or an online tutorial (perhaps with graphics, video, audio or a

> **Tip**
>
> Divide your FAQs into subject areas to make it easier for your visitor to navigate and get to the relevant question. If, for instance, you are providing a set of FAQs on your local soccer team, you could divide this into:
>
> - Questions about tickets
> - Questions about location
> - Questions about membership
> - Questions about players and personalities

virtual tutor). You may wish to provide a set of FAQs - frequently asked questions. These are very useful for your visitors, especially if you can anticipate their likely queries or concerns.

Warning! If you do offer telephone support, remember that people may be calling you from any part of the world at any time so unless you're able to offer a 24-7 service in several world languages, don't offer what you can't deliver.

A note about copyright

You may be tempted to add content to your site by taking in other sites. Don't do this without permission. You may be breaching copyright laws (it's not true that anything on the internet is copyright free). But provided you ask nicely, and maybe can give something in return, you may find that the owner of the content is quite happy to let you use it, provided that you give links to his site or at least acknowledgement of its source. If you're lucky, you may come across content that states that it is copyright free, in which case you are able to use it. Copyrighter on the internet is a tricky subject and is best left to professional legal advice if you have any doubts. And don't forget that this applies equally to photographs, text, logos, graphics - even branded fonts and colour schemes.

Brainstorm your content ideas

This is a paper and pencil task. You should thoroughly think through what you want to include in your web site before spending money on costly designers, web builders or do-it-yourself software.

Divide your content into A-list, B-list, C-list (and maybe more). A-list content should include all essential bits of information. B-list is important but not so essential, C-list - useful to have but not essential information etc.

Your A-list content may include: Contact details, what you do, products and services, aims and objectives.

B-list might involve technical information, a mission statement, company profile (Who's who in the organisation may be with photographs).

C-list categories might include what customers think, archive material, upcoming events etc.

Site content is all about value added - the more relevant links you have, the more useful it is for visitors to come to the site. That doesn't mean you should include every link you can think of. Don't include people in competition with your site that are likely to give you a bad name, especially if they contain content of a dubious nature or contradict the image you're trying to convey. For instance, if

> **Tip**
>
> You can learn a lot about content by looking at web sites that are similar to yours or are in your line of business or activity. If you are a school, voluntary organisation or club, take a look at what the others are doing. What's in their A-list? What have they left out that you should include?

you're trying to sell ethically traded products, you should think twice about giving links to politically incorrect sites.

Think of the link as a service to your customer or user. What would he or she find useful? What would make the visit to my site even more valuable? What link can I give them that will provide an unexpected service or benefit? What link site will I be happy recommending to my users?

Of course, if your site is successful, you can expect other sites to want to link with yours. In any case, it's always a good idea to check with site owners that everyone is happy to be used as a link, as there needs to be a reciprocal advantage. So before you let people link into your site, make sure you're happy that their image and content sits well with yours. After all, do you want to be recommended by a site that may be perceived to be not very professional? You don't want to be tarred with the same brush as someone who fails to meet your standards. So be very careful in planning your links and any reciprocal links.

Email links

You can turn some links into an email link so that when the visitor clicks on them, up pops his favourite email program with a blank message window and your email address already in place in the send to box. It's a good idea to make the email links clear. So you might say something like 'Tell us what you think' or 'Send us your query.' These email links can be fantastically useful for the visitor but use them sparingly.

Graphics

When or why not to use graphics is very much a matter of taste. Graphics liven up a web page and these days a text only page would be very unusual. But there are those, including some of the top web designers, who support clean, simple text pages with the minimum of graphics and images. In the end, it comes down to your personal taste and what you think your visitors will like.

Chapter 6

Making a visual impact

Chapter 6

Making a visual impact

Summary

· How to design your web site
· Navigating around the site
· What you need to know about graphics and colour

A web site is no different from your business card, your letterheads, your organisation's logo, your corporate colour scheme and your brand identity. It needs above all to be consistent. Visitors need to feel confident that as they surf through your site the visual cues are telling them that they're still in the right place. That means each page you build should have consistency of colour, layout, font, general structure. Imagine clicking onto a page on your site to find that the whole layout, font size and character, and colour scheme has changed. Visitors would feel insecure and wonder if they've strayed into someone else's site. That doesn't mean that each page needs to look exactly the same - far from it. But if, for instance, the pages use frames* to keep their text and images together, it's a bit worrying to click into a new page that has no frames.

*Pages on the web can be divided into frames or tables. A frame allows a section of the web pages to stay the same while other parts change. You might put your logo, or navigation bars in a frame so that they stay there whatever pages your visitors are on. There's a lot to learn about frames that you need to know if you decide to build your own site and learn HTML code. One useful feature is linking frames, which mean that as you click on buttons in one frame - say an introductory menu - another set of buttons pops up. You can also link frames together so that a command in one frame will change another. This helps a site to be much more interactive and user-defined. There are some disadvantages of frames, however - they can be slowish to load and not all browsers can deal with them (although this is less and less true).

Tables are the basic building blocks of any web site. Like any table, an HTML table is a series of rows and columns into which all kinds of information can be put including columns of text, graphics and headings. Tables are used to line up all the content of the page so that it looks well ordered and in line. See any book on web building for more on this.

Your web site needs to reflect the image that you have already established or wish to establish. So your web site needs to make an impact and confirm the image that people expect from you. It needs to be attractive but appropriate for your organisation. And you know best what image you're trying to convey. Think about this before you unleash the talents of an eager web designer who may want to play with all the latest fancy graphics, fonts, images,

> **Tip**
>
> When you are planning your site, make a rough drawing of what each page should look like in terms of layout, colour, text fonts and graphics. You can stray from the plan as the site develops but if you start consistent you'll stay consistent.

animations or groovy colour schemes. The over-enthusiastic web designer is just as much a nuisance as a completely incompetent one (and unfortunately there are plenty of both breeds out there). So what should you avoid? Well, if you intend to present a highly professional image, then please put a complete ban on:

- horribly old-fashioned fonts (courier comes to mind);

- cheery, over-familiar text such as 'Hi guys - so cool you could come to my site. Let me offer you the latest in a high quality jewellery';

- title bars and text boxes which have been drawn from cheap and nasty software tools last updated in the early 90s;

- clip art (most of it is naff and hateful). The worst offenders are those terrible categories you get with clip art - vehicles, electrical goods, greetings. They all seem to be created by a talentless would-be artist who has nothing more than a blunt pencil to draw with;

- horribly old-fashioned and boxy bullets - squares, diamonds and worst of all ticks and crosses;

- complete absence of colour - yes, there are still some monochrome web sites out there;

- blinking pages (this should be a capital offence);

- huge images that take ages to load - even worse, when the images are totally irrelevant to the subject of the page or do nothing to enhance it.

Tip

Make an image pay its way - don't let it in there too easily. Put it through a grilling. Why are you here? Are you worth waiting for? Isn't there any other way of making the point? The problem is that if the user has a slow modem (say connecting at less than 33.6 khps) then a 100 kilobytes image will take half a minute or more to load. That is plenty of time to get fed up and move on (just try staring at this page and doing nothing for 30 seconds - boring isn't it?) Remember that the average surfer will move on unless something happens to his screen in less than ten seconds. That means a user with a slow modem connection speed will only accept images with a file size less than 25 kbs. Of course, if the user is requested to click on an image, then he may be more willing to wait - at least it's his choice and you've told him why it's worth waiting for.

Other hungry users of file space include video clips, sound files and animated graphics. It's not to say that these elements aren't useful: They can add tremendous interest to a page and bring alive your site. Imagine using a video clip to show what you can do. Think of a trainer or consultant in full flight with his audience, or how about some customer recommendations from the horse's mouth. Imagine the power of an audio clip to show what a bunch of musicians can do or showing off the choral abilities of your local choir to promote your own CD. But before you get carried away, remember that what may be music to someone's ears, may be a hellish cacophony to others. A lot of people really hate music that blares out as soon as a site is opened up. This can be really tacky.

You could use an animated graphic to illustrate how you might build a model. As you can see, the possibilities are endless. But, these files can be very slow to load where a user has a slow modem, a computer with limited memory or processor power, or is trying to download your site when traffic is busy. The internet may be powerful, but you don't

> **Tip**
>
> Sound files should only be included where they are an integral part of the product, service or idea on offer. If it's important to hear the boss's annual statement then by all means include a sound clip. Use it sparingly!

have the power over your users. Of course if you're sure that your likely visitors have the latest broadband connections and super-fast processors in their state-of-the-art PCs or Apple Macs, then you can get away with these file hungry elements.

Navigating around the site

A web site should be like a well ordered home, office or (if your scale is grand) palace. It should be attractive but easy to find your way around. Don't make your web site a maze - visitors will not thank you for setting them challenges in orientation or hide and seek. Navigating around the site is a key to success as visitors moving around the site should be completely natural, where a click of a mouse button is done without thought.

The three-click rule

All the content on your site should be accessible within three clicks of the home page. Here's a simple example of a web site devoted to a catering service:

Home page includes a brief description of the business and several buttons that offer:

Sample menus

Delivery

FAQs

A click on Sample Menus takes you to a range of options with further clicks taking you to:

Special events

Special dietary needs

A click on special events takes you to:

Weddings

Birthday parties

Anniversaries

So if visitors are likely to want to know about a wedding reception, three clicks takes them to the nitty gritty. Notice that the key to this is a logical series of steps that the visitor is likely to take. We've said it before, but we can't say it often enough: KNOW YOUR VISITORS.

The three-click rule isn't the only show in town. Consider:

The rule of five

This says that complex, multi-layered menus offering more than five main choices tend to confuse web users.

Take a look at a good department store web site. It must be very tempting for them to offer a page for each department and sub menus galore for each group of products within each, and sub-sub menus for each product within the group. If the logical flow is clear, and REFLECTS the way shoppers use the actual (as opposed to virtual) store, then a rule of 10, 20 or more may be perfectly acceptable. Take a look at the excellent www.tesco.com.

Tesco is one of the UK's biggest supermarkets and leads the way on internet shopping. See how quickly you can get to a product of your choice (I went for Australian wines). You're there in about five clicks or fewer. Notice also the CONSISTENCY of design. Each page has the menu bar clearly visible on the left (very little scrolling needed on my tiny screen anyway) and that means you can get back to the home page easily. Notice also the clear brand image and the ever-so simple black text on white background format (the old ones are the best ones). Hats off also to www.johnlewis.com for another no-fuss, highly professional site. I got to the digital camera I wanted to learn more about in three clicks from the home page. Well done! (And again, notice the nice simple layouts and clear, clear text).

One really golden rule is: When in doubt, leave it out. Be minimalist. Err on the side of extreme caution. You can always add pages if you've overdone the concision. Don't treat your web site as a standard brochure or catalogue. It can't really replace the giant shopping catalogues. The best sites allow some kind of interactivity between the seller and the buyer. And there's always a feedback form to allow your visitors to give their opinions.

Another golden(ish) rule is to get the home page up and running without any more clicks. Don't ask visitors to 'Click here' or 'Click the icon' or 'Find the map, look for the dragon and click on his tail.' This is called a 'splash screen' and is for professional purposes little more than an annoyance. Of course it may be necessary to have this screen if you want users to sign in as members or state they are over 18 or some other requirement. You may WANT to slow them down. As long as you are aware that a Splash Screen will delay access into the site, then fine. It may fit in with your requirements.

Helping your users to navigate around the site

It all comes down to planning. You should organise your content so that users can get around the site easily and logically. Start with lots of sheets of paper. Work out your A-list, B-list etc content and put it all into a logical order; an order that you would expect a user to follow (remember the more you can get into the head of your user, the more effective your site will be.

Think about the questions your user may ask:

Why have I come to this site?

What will I expect to discover?

What does this organisation offer me?

Which product, service, and department do I need?

What do I need to know?

What extra information do I need?

What do I need next?

Where do I need to go now?

How do I get back? How do I contact this organisation?

> **Tip**
>
> Draw a flow chart taking the user from the home page right through your site. Think about the logical progression through the site and how the user can find the way back. If you're going to use external links, think where they might come. Be prepared to do many different versions of this flow chart and to discuss it with lots of people including your web designer.

If you decide to design and build your own site, make sure you organise your file that makes up the site in a simple and logical way. Create different folders for main topics, images, sound files, photographs, files to download and PDF format files (special text files which can hold very large amounts of copy - you can even have a whole book in one PDF file).

If the site is quite large, you may wish to create sub folders that will branch off from the main topic folders. For instance, if you have a folder marked 'Australia' you can divide this into sub folders for each state e.g. Australia/Victoria. You may wish to create further sub folders e.g. Australia/Victoria/Melbourne/cafés and so on. Although all this is really for the web builders, thinking in terms of folders and sub folders will help you organise your contents material.

What you need to know about graphics and colour

Although this is not a book about design, it is useful to know some of the key principles - and the questions to ask your web designer.

Will all web site visitors be able to see the graphics? It's possible that what is visible in one browser is not visible in another. Also users do have the option of turning graphics off. And don't forget some people might be looking at your web site on a WAP phone, PDA (hand-held computer) which means that the graphic would be very small.

Will images or photographs take a long time to load? Images are usually in GIF or JPEG format - the latter is a highly compressed file that is especially suitable for complex graphics and photographs.

Navigation bars

How can you help your visitors get to where they want to be in three, four, or five clicks? The best way is to design a navigation bar. This is a row of text links or buttons that are placed vertically or horizontally on each page. Most web sites, but not all, place their navigation bar on top of the page, or down the left-hand side. If you're using buttons, make them clear so that the text associated with them can be easily read. Some over enthusiastic designers hate the thought of plain old text in the navigation bars, but there's absolutely nothing wrong with this. Text only can be very powerful, although a whole page of listed text links could be tiring on the eyes. You can also afford to be inventive. Have a look, for instance, at the site for World Society for the Protection of Animals - www.wspa.org.au.

Notice the use of appropriate graphics - in this case animal symbols within a rounded text box making it clear how the user can get from one page to another. Notice also how the site has a nice mixture of text links and larger image links on the right hand side of the home page. The clever use of visuals makes the site not only easy to navigate but attractive to look at.

Another common device in designing navigation bars is the use of tabs sitting horizontally along the top of the page. These tabs, used in conjunction with vertical navigation bars, can indicate main subject areas.

Imagine that you were designing a site for a social club. You may decide to put all the main sections of the club in a horizontal navigation bar at the top of the page and subdivisions of each page down a vertical bar on the left. Let's say this is the page for events.

home	bar	events	Xmas	sport	trips

Elvis night

Halloween

Games night

Quiz

The Xmas page navigation bars might look lie this:

home	bar	events	Xmas	sport	trips

Party

Santa

Carols

Charity

The top bar stays the same throughout the site so that the user can quickly and easily navigate around the main activities of the club. Notice that 'Home' appears on each page so that the user can always get back to the start.

You may, of course, equally decide to put the permanent categories on the left vertical bar and the details for each section on the top horizontal. You'll see an example of this at the RAC site. Look at one of its sections, e.g. on hotels, at www.rac.co.uk/hotels.

Notice that the stuff that's on each page is down on the left, and the categories within each department are on the top bar (indicated by a simple arrow link). Notice also how each page looks consistent and is badged in the RAC colours.

At the top of the page is a link to a 'site map.' If you're planning on a big site with lots of pages and sectors, this is a good idea. A site map is a visual index of every section and subsection on the site. It's great to help people out if they got a big lost.

There's another very nice site at the government's Inland Revenue page at www.inlandrevenue.gov.uk/index.htm.

Being a huge subject, the challenges of getting everything on the site must have been daunting, but there are useful lessons to be learnt in the execution of the site:

- The colour scheme is calming and welcoming.

- The text is very clear.

- There are navigation bars along the top horizontal: index, help and search.

- Down the left side, there are the main categories of tax payers (clients).

- Down the right hand side, there is lots of useful stuff about taxes, publications, jobs, forms and anything else.

- The main body of text in the middle is packed with links to main topical stories. Notice also the two opportunities to search the site - along the top horizontal AND in the side bar.

Chapter 7

Writing for your site

Chapter 7

Writing for your site

Summary

· Some basic examples of written English
· Writing tips
· Maintaining your site

A web site is not a book or a magazine. You don't read a web site in the same way. You don't explore a web site (usually) by starting at the home page, scrolling down to the end, going on to page two and following the site in a linear fashion.

A web site is a whole new way of reading. It empowers the reader to pick and choose where to go next - forward, back or sideways. Provided the navigation around the site is clear, users can enjoy creating their own sequential tour around the site. So forget beginning, middle and end. A web site doesn't work like that.

All this has an impact on the way a web site should be written. Every page should follow the CIR rule:

C - clarity

I - impact

R - relevance

Because of its non-linear nature, a web site has to work on every individual page. Actually, not just every page but every screen shot. Remember that your page may run into several screens and require scrolling. Also, because the medium empowers the user to such an extent, you can't be sure that they will view the site in any particular order. So, each screen must make an impact, be clear in its intention and its ability to be understood, and be relevant to the needs of the user.

One of the first rules of writing is to know your audience. The written style that your web site contains must appeal to the user. As we keep saying, the more you know about your visitors, the more you can target the correct style. It's best to write as though you're addressing a specific individual - have that person in mind as you create the text. So, think about your readers' preferences. Here are your options:

> ### Tip
>
> Before your web site goes live, check each page for CIR.
>
> Text or graphics? These are not mutually exclusive and you should choose a combination of the two to make your point as clear as possible. The old adage that a picture is worth a thousand words is true, but don't overdose on the visuals.

- Very informal, friendly, chatty style (it may be your style, but is it theirs?) This may be fine for a children's or youth audience, or in a club where each visitor is known.

- An informal but less direct style i.e. the language you use is simple and colloquial but not over familiar.

- An informal but more official style i.e. the language is clear and simple and takes an authoritative tone - the kind of letter you get these days from your bank manager.

- Formal but engaged with the reader i.e. clearly addressing the reader but using language which is possibly technical, legalistic, precise.

- Formal but detached - not directly addressing the reader. This style could include a list of rules and regulations, laws, academic text.

Here are some examples:

Informal and chatty:

'Hi guys! Welcome to our cool new site. We're gonna have buckets of fun.'

Informal but slightly detached:

'Hello. It's good to welcome you to our new site. It's fun and we hope you enjoy it.'

Informal but less direct:

'Welcome to our new site. It's designed to be enjoyed.'

Informal but authoritative:

'On behalf of Acme Web Holdings, the board would like to welcome all visitors.'

Formal but detached:

'The board of Acme Web Holdings have issued a statement supporting the wish that site visitors shall be offered appropriate salutations (OK this may be a bit over the top but you see what we mean).'

Your choice of style depends not only on your audience, but also the function of the page. Styles can of course vary within a site:

- Informal and friendly for a home page.

- More authoritative for pages dealing in your products or services.

- Very formal in pages which outline legal or other obligations.

There is no special rule about writing for the web except that the style should be appropriate. Your written English should be clear and accurate. There are lots of books that will give advice on written English (there's an excellent one by Susannah Ross, *A simple guide to writing for your web site*, Prentice Hall, 2001).

Some basic rules of written English

Never use ten words when one will do. Because the screen is so small, you have to make every word count. No waffle! When you have written a first draft of your text go over it and edit it - be brutal, kick out unnecessary words or phrases. Be savage with any repetitions.

Use simple words instead of more formal ones:

Formal words	Simple words
purchase	buy
inform	tell
commence	begin
requirements	needs

Avoid tautology - unnecessary words. Some of the classics include: 'past history' (all history is in the past), 'the reason is because…'

Avoid unnecessary phrases - a common error indicating that too little time was taken on editing the text. Here's an example:

Before:

'As we all know, there is a fine line that can be drawn between a quality product and one that is good but not up to scratch. We at Acme Tool Kits believe, and we are sincere about this, that our products are second to none in regard to quality, durability and in the general standard of our workmanship, for which we are truly proud.'

After:

'Acme Tool Kits are durable. We are proud that none can beat us for quality and workmanship.'

Notice that the paragraph also starts with the main point. Writing for the web is like journalism. You have a very limited space so your text must grab attention from the start and be interesting and relevant.

Passive language

'Parents will be given an introductory tour on arrival at the school.'

Turn this into active language:

'We will give parents an introductory tour of the school as they arrive.'

A passive style - detached and lacking the personal touch - may be acceptable for formal occasions but in general try to avoid it. The web is a very personal medium. It is like a two-way conversation and therefore you should try to identify yourself and the user in the language you use.

> ### Tip
>
> Always edit your text (at least three times) and if possible, get someone really fussy about written style to check it over. Cut, cut and cut again. Make ten words do what 50 have tried.
>
> Say no to:
>
> - jargon and slang (unless you think it appropriate for your audience);
>
> - clichés such as 'high as a kite' or 'she was literally too far gone' or 'we were sick as a parrot;' the English language is full of clichés like this - be aware of them and; they take up a lot of space, are signs of lazy writing and give a poor impression.

More writing tips

Justify your text to the left - it's easier to read than centred, right or justified.

Use a sans serif font (such as Arial or Comic Sans MS) for short paragraphs. Where the text is denser, consider using a serif font like Times New Roman or New York. Serif fonts can be easier to read where there is a lot of text to handle on one screen. The final choice comes down to looking carefully at how your site looks on a monitor. Experiment with different fonts.

Use short sentences - if possible one that takes up one or two lines at most. The web is not the place for complex sub-clauses.

Use bullet points to break up the text and make your points very succinctly. One of the benefits of bullet points is that you don't have to stick to conventions of grammar. You can write in a headline mode.

So instead of:

'There are three types of membership of our club. Gold membership entitles the holder to free entry at all times and a complimentary glass of wine. Silver membership allows you to enjoy club facilities at weekends without charge. Bronze membership means that you can gain free access to our club on one weekday per week.'

Using bullet points:

'**Membership**

- Gold - free entry without restriction and a complimentary glass of wine

- Silver - weekends free

- Bronze - one weekday per week, free entry'

You shouldn't overdo bullet points but they're a good way to get over lots of information. Of course, you could use each as a hyperlink so that the user can find more information about each point by clicking on the bullet.

Position your text carefully on the screen

You will have only around half (or less) of the screen to write in. Navigation bars, menus, other links and so on take up the rest. That means that each page should have no more than 200 words of text, depending on your font size. With headings it may be much less than this.

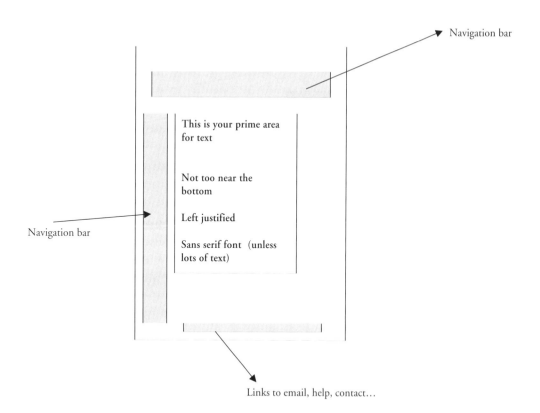

Navigation bar

This is your prime area for text

Not too near the bottom

Left justified

Sans serif font (unless lots of text)

Navigation bar

Links to email, help, contact...

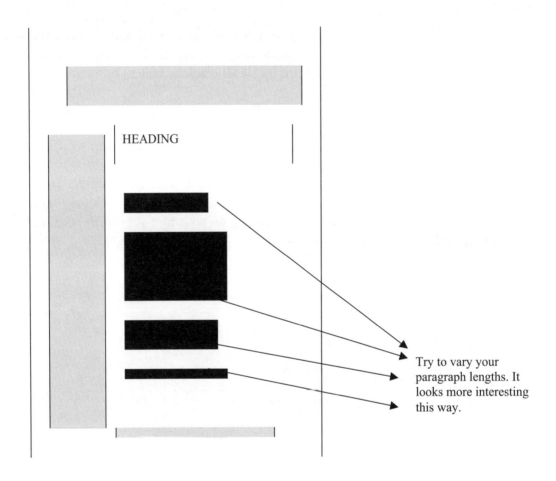

HEADING

Try to vary your paragraph lengths. It looks more interesting this way.

Embed some of your links within the text. If done sparingly, this can be a very powerful way of creating text that is uniquely web-wise. What other medium could allow you to instantly jump to another topic? Links within a text usually appear as a simple underline. Click on the word, and get to a related page.

Don't overwrite the home page. It is tempting to pack all you want to say on the home page. With hyperlinks this is not necessary, but don't say too little either. Lead the user into the site and put something in your text that is appealing, attractive and attention grabbing.

So, if your site is all about collecting rare china tea services start your home page with something like:

'Everything for the collector of rare china tea services.

We have teapots to make you drool.

The world's rarest milk jug?

Offer of the week.

News from the teapot fair.'

All these act as a 'come on' to tempt people to explore further.

Maintaining your site

A web site is a dynamic tool. Unless its content is constantly changing and being updated, the site can quickly become moribund. Nothing turns off potential visitors more than a tired, predictable, and out of date web site. You can still see commercial web sites that tell you they were last updated a year or more ago. What good are they? And what kind of message are they giving if the webmasters can't be bothered to put fresh new content to the site. Updating your site cannot be done without cost. It will have to be maintained and to be frank that can be a lot of work. Of course, if you hire a web consultant to do the donkeywork, your task is easy.

Maintaining your site may involve:

- Adding fresh new content - depending on the function of your site. You might have to do this every day.

- Improving layout and navigation - there is no such thing as the perfect site and there's always something to improve, especially if you're getting negative feedback from your clients or visitors. One of the most common complaints is that despite the best efforts, people can't find their way around the site or back to the home page, or other pages.

- Improving the facilities on site - adding new features, speeding up navigation and so on.

- Checking that everything works properly - especially links to other pages or sites. There's nothing more annoying than clicking on a link that goes nowhere (perhaps the site you are linking to has gone out of business). So it is a really important job to make sure that all links are live.

What the experts think

Re-evaluate a site's overall design and colour scheme regularly. Check the mechanics of your site. There is nothing worse than launching a site only to be tapped on the shoulder by your mate and told pompously that those funky links are directing the user to a typical error404 page! This means those pages that your site is linked to no longer exist and you've been told by your standard browser error page! So if you must have errors, design the pages with a personal error message. Half the users out there don't know what error404 is! Think of an alternative such as: 'We apologise for the inconvenience…and hopefully the problem will be rectified shortly.' A personal message in line with your design will read better then the typical jargon.

Also, be aware of contact numbers off by one-digit and email addresses that no longer exist.

Our advice is not to launch unless you've checked your site thoroughly. And if you already have, remember to check it regularly. A full makeover is usually performed every 4-6 months. It really does pay to keep your site fresh!

Chapter 8

Security

Chapter 8

Security

Summary

· Malicious viruses
· The script kiddies vs. Computer systems experts
· Big boy fraudster!

Security issues in web technologies have been baffling users and professionals for many years. It is one of the most important issues surrounding web technologies to date, and one that deserves yet another publication on its own. As the computers of the world, and the users of today become more and more connected, security becomes more and more of an issue. As a user and a self-respecting web entrepreneur (assuming that you are!), we will guide you gently through the cyber maze and introduce you to some brief thoughts on what to think about when developing a security plan for your site. The most common issues we are all aware of. However, for reference sake we will include only the most common issues below.

Given the complex nature of the problem, and your steadily growing fears about launching your very own site, you are strongly advised to leave security to a responsible professional. You need to be aware that internet crime is rife within the industry and will continue to remain so. The uninitiated are at particular risk and here we can see the truth of the old adage that a little knowledge is a dangerous thing! A blasé and arrogant assumption that because you can type 60 words a minute and know your way around Outlook Express blindfolded means you can tackle your own security issues is a sure fire recipe to ending up out of pocket. There is a need to set computer security policies and procedures for sites that have systems on the internet or not on the internet. That need is most definitely better left to a professional to meet.

Common issues

1. Malicious viruses

Malicious viruses are common and they are a problem. The damages that a sophisticated virus can incur are many, great and costly, and you must protect yourself against them. Run virus protection software! No one, except fools and liars, will claim that any one virus protection software is 100 per cent secure, but having one is surely better than no security at all?

The two big suppliers, which you may well have come across, are McAfee, Dr Soloman VirusScan and Symantec's 'Norton AntiVirus' who offer evaluation versions prior to purchasing one of the many packages. Note that there are other really good alternatives. Go search and utilise that available function - the search engine! Given the recent boom scare in the distribution of these deathly viruses it would 'pay' to look into it!

Email is the most dangerous hazard our intrepid cyber surfers face and its associated email attachments. Sophisticated viruses can easily open personal address lists and send themselves on! Is the title of the mail out of character? Is the content short and impersonal? Check it out and exercise extreme caution. Is it from a known contact or acquaintance or someone you've never heard of? Be careful!

Take great care, obviously, in downloading from sites. That game you thought so funky might very well be deadly. In addition, anything that runs a separate program or needs some kind of installation procedure is usually an executable and needs to be dealt with carefully. An executable can destroy a computer in seconds given it has direct access to the core of your computer. Many downloads are in zip format - watch for the malicious executable (.exe extension) disguised as such.

2. The script kiddies vs. Computer systems experts

There are opposing views as to whether the two are the same. Personal experience has reaffirmed the truth that crackers can be defined as 'Script kiddies' and hackers as 'Computer systems experts.' However, the common definition is that computer experts breach computer security of networks, web and email servers. They identify the weaknesses of a system and then exploit those weaknesses. Funky as the culture may seem, the problem lies in them having to protect their anonymity!

To protect their anonymity, they build programs called Trojans, the binary rather than the rubber variety by the way, and backdoors, which are disguised as games or some other kind of executable programs. Our ever-reliable media has distorted once again the issue and characterised the two to be one and the same. Truth be known, not all Trojans are backdoors and vice-versa. At best - they will send back some personal information about you. At worst - they have the ability to remote control your machine to the point of destroying your computer!

To avoid getting a Trojan and backdoor program into your system, start with a good piece of virus protection software (which will avoid 90 per cent of Trojans and backdoors ever getting in) and then consider a firewall (which will stop any of them getting out should you be so unlucky they ever get in!) Users and companies should buy one of the third party firewalls, however cheap. This will stop 99.9 per cent of the 'cracker and hacker culture' but it is not fool proof. Nothing on the internet is fool proof - we wish we could tell you otherwise but we don't tell lies!

3. Big boy fraudster!

Internet fraud is booming. The fraud rate for online transactions is 24 times higher than it is offline! And guess what? Your customers rarely find themselves liable for internet fraud as the merchants and credit-card companies swallow the debt! So it's not you who incurs the debt. That careless shrug of the shoulders is common these days given the number of cowboys in the web profit-making game. Just remember, it is your reputation in tatters. It is your reputation that reflects on your business online and offline. Remember the hard won integrity you gleaned a while ago? Well it's now kissing itself goodbye as it sinks away down the toilet! Take the appropriate steps in providing adequate security for your customers, as no one likes a cowboy!

Secure Sockets Layer (SSL) is a coding method that's extremely hard to crack! A 'must have' given you have directed your attention to a web-based profit-making site. Hopefully it will mean that all your users' personal details will be encoded, and will travel safely down the wire. Fraud is a serious problem associated with real-time online transaction processing and is part of a total package that needs to be thoroughly researched, should this be one of your main business objectives.

The threat is there, it is prominent in the internet culture and it lurks ready to pounce when we least expect it. It mysteriously cloaks, it never disappears and it has no identity. Don't take the cheap route. Don't take the risk. Nervous about security? So are your customers! Should you decide to launch a site, don't be a dummy, Leave security to the professionals.

Consider:

1. **What are you trying to protect?**

Risk analysis involves determining what it is you are trying to protect. Those valuable assets should include hardware, software, data, people, documentation and supplies…oh and the most obvious…the security server itself whose access we hope is both minimum and accessible from on-site only!

2. **Who do you need to protect them from?**

Identify the threats. Who has unauthorised access to resources and/or information? Is your business a risk in the internet culture?

3.   How would you protect it?

This is a long and involved process but well worth it in the end given efforts spent on security yield cost effective benefits. Would you authorise certain personnel to have access to certain information? And subsequently, allocate them passwords or keys with encryption? Would you think about protecting your networking and infrastructure? How about protecting those internal networks and external available services?

A full and detailed assessment involves effort and an understanding of standard security measures that hopefully businesses adhere to. There is a need to look ahead. A great deal of publicity surrounds those intruders who seemingly worm their way anonymously into niches and crannies causing total havoc within an organisation. It must be said, however, that 'hackers' focus on multi-national organisations as opposed to the wee ones. But there is a need for your business to assess the risk factors associated with the industry. Were you also aware that the actual loss a business faces is from the inside as opposed to the outside? Given this scenario, can you determine how likely the threats are internally?

Implement measures that will protect your assets in a cost effective way and review this process on a regular basis. There will always be a weakness, thus always room for improvements. Internet security and its associated polices grow in their complexity and are evolving rapidly. Again, a well recommended professional would provide you with all the facts, options and choices and help you evaluate accordingly.

Having thought of these two alternatives: 'deny all, allow all,' the choice between them will depend on the nature and function of the site itself and its need for security.

Chapter 9

Using your web site as part of your marketing strategy

Chapter 9

Using your web site as part of your marketing strategy

Summary

· Your business objectives
· Is your web site database oriented or profit making?
· How to build good customer relations

To properly compete within the niche market or to out-perform a competitor, a strategic marketing plan should be devised.

Key elements of a web-based marketing plan

What are your business objectives? Why do you want a web site?

There is no reason at all why your site cannot be multi-faceted. Indeed, the most successful ones often are but equally valuable are sites that allow you to do what you do best. Only you know what that is, but you need to be clear on several things.

Is it database oriented?

Maybe your site is a source of information for customers and internally for staff. For example, field sales personnel, with the aid of a password or key code, can access your site for the latest price movements in your products and those of your home and overseas competitors. Your sales executives can from the field be constantly in touch with market fluctuations or new benefits you are able to provide. Or you might be a school that uses the site to access key records such as past exam results, internal memos, governors' reports, parent-teacher AGMs - or even the script from last year's nativity play.

Keeping current in this way is a superb way of supporting your staff with the very latest they have to offer your clients. In this case avoid glitzy graphics and concentrate on simple layout with any relevant facts and figures easily and sensibly displayed and arranged for the easiest of use.

Possibly your site is little more than an online catalogue. That's OK too. Clients looking for price and availability can avoid those agonising telephone queues and the ubiquitous Casio concerti and with three clicks get straight to your page with the latest price, availability and any discount they may qualify for. A click or two more and their order is 'in the bag.'

Maybe your site does all of these things plus another 27 functions,. Great! No problem! All is possible with the complete web-based solutions package available from a reputable and skilled outfit.

Is it profit making?

Online sales, advertising space on your site, credit card access to your site and just about any method you can devise can be assembled to ensure your sites primary purpose is the generation of profit.

Do you want to build good customer relations?

Excellent features of some sites are those that provide a significant focus on customer feedback. No one is suggesting that you have a cheesy guest book, which your reluctant clients are strong-armed into signing, but consider for a moment, if you will, the benefits of closer relations with your client base. Your site can easily accommodate a host of features that allow your clients interactive and proactive relations with your business.

The feedback form to build better customer relations?

Feedback forms are excellent examples of utilising a simple hosting function. Although not new to the 'wacky web,' they provide a means for you to acquire relevant customer and potential customer details. A handy database of collated details beneficial to you. The trick is to get the correct information and pertain it to your business objectives. If used responsibly it can be a beneficial marketing tool, giving you collected details of hopefully one of your targeted audiences. However, it must be said that a great many sites provide a quality feedback form that will also include a privacy policy, and one that constantly reaffirms that all personal details will remain confidential.

The electronic newsletter to build better customer relations?

The electronic newsletter (or e-zine as it's commonly known) is again an old marketing tool employed by web marketing enthusiasts for years. It provides an opportunity for you to stay in touch with customers and potential customers given its subscription and deliverance on a weekly, fortnightly or monthly basis. Feedback on your chosen e-zine is an important factor and one that needs to be taken into consideration should you decide on the 'e-zine tactic.' Remember, the content needs to be fresh on delivery - stale and outdated content will lose you subscriptions. Given the number of e-zines on the web at the moment, this is something you can do without! New articles! New exposures! New anything, but relevant to your key objective! Get your audience involved by making sure the ezine's content is directed towards them and provide them with an insight they won't find anywhere else.

In the early days, when moneymaking web enthusiasts explored the concept of making money on the internet, the e-zine culture was hit heavily from all angles. Given its potential at the time and the marketing 'budding' web entrepreneurs who saw this as a way of cutting down on conventional means of advertising (which were and still are costly), the culture bloated. To have an e-zine would mean to be in an industry whose audience would benefit. For example, a freelance writer and/or publishing company could distribute tasty samples of their work before stating their main objective, which would be 'To buy, to purchase - click here!' I hope this example explains the e-zine culture clearly. To use e-zine as a secondary medium of advertising, given your first medium, will be a move back to the more conventional and offline means of advertising. Use the TV, radio, newspapers and industry magazines! Draw your target audience to your site first and then convince them to subscribe and/or purchase.

Increase customer loyalty?

There is not much more on the face of the earth that is as valuable as loyal customers. How about using your site to reward that loyalty and, of course, to ensure it remains the constant, priceless currency it has always been? Maybe the select, blue chip clients in your database get that VIP treatment, such as a password qualifying them for special discounts or a better courier or delivery service? A site can certainly be a seriously powerful psychological tool in cementing, consolidating and deepening the bond that exists between you and the men and women that really matter to your business.

Focus on customer satisfaction?

Maybe we are at risk of repeating the points made above here but humour me OK? I mean let's face it, the satisfied customer is the customer that places his business with you so it makes sense for you to ensure your client base is as satisfied as it is possible for you to make them. Use your site to make it happen! A competent, reputable, professional solutions outfit can easily show you how. Still, if your clients seem to like too much investment for all this hard work, there is always the *Evening News*!

Chapter 10

Using your web site to maintain the edge

Chapter 10

Using your web site to maintain the edge

Summary

· Learning from your competitors
· Banner and traditional advertising
· Reciprocal linking and search engine strategies
· The future now!
· References

Once you have a web site, you may want people to come to you rather than anyone else. That means giving your site real value to the user. Here are some ideas that should put your site high up in people's preferences.

1. Making the most of links

Links can be arranged on your site to the FTSE and other markets for your clients to make up to the minute decisions on the state of their business and their financial status from the comfort of your site. Make it easy for them to place their business with you. Why have them visiting three or four or more web sites before having the hassle of logging back onto yours? Who knows, they may find somewhere else along the way to leave their orders!

2. Learn from your competitors

It's a pretty safe bet that if your opposition doesn't have a site by now, then it isn't going to be too much longer before they do! You don't need anyone to spell out for you the obvious pitfalls of your rivals having an edge on you. But why not look at this from a slightly different angle? Take a look at your clients' sites, see what might work for you, check out those mistakes that make your toes curl and see what you could do and improve upon. It always makes sense to keep tabs on the competition. Looking at their sites gives you the opportunity of looking directly at your competition and seeing the benefits of them harnessing the most powerful sales and marketing tool since Alexander Graham Bell thought the phone might be a great idea!

3. Banner advertising

Go to many web sites (especially commercial ones but increasingly those involved in the public or voluntary sector too) and you are bound to see at least one 'banner.' These are advertisements that are displayed as your web site is loaded. Some Internet Service Providers (ISPs) offer a cheaper domain hosting service as long as you let them

> **Tip**
>
> If you have a good working relationship with another organisation, consider running their banner as an exchange for yours. There should be mutual interest involved and the visitor should see that there is a clear link between your organisation's offer and the one from the banner company.

display their banners on your site. You may also be tempted to take a banner advertisement from another organisation on to your site. There may be temptations such as the cheesy, 'you display my banner and I'll display yours,' or apparently tempting offers to pay you 1p (or less) per click! So 20-50 clicks later and 12 months of waiting for that 20-50 pence cheque to arrive in the post, has it all been worth it? You now not only have a cheesy reputation but visitors and potential visitors avoid you like the plague because they hate your intrusive banners.

To be fair though, banner advertising with existing and potential customers can be beneficial. The whole concept just has a bad name attached to it. There is absolutely nothing wrong with exchanging banners with those external resources that you have good relations with offline! In this sense, it is most advantageous.

If you have a good working relationship with another organisation, consider running their banner as an exchange for yours. There should be mutual interest involved and the visitor should see that there is a clear link between your organisation's offer and the one from the banner company.

What the experts think

So you've decided on an APPROPRIATE banner exchange? Size ought to be small - avoid the A4 width ones like the plague. You need a banner that will grab the attention of a viewer in seconds! Please try to design it tastefully? Effective colours, even in the 21st century, remain bright, bold and cheerful and animation is quick and fast…or not. If you must, mediate between the two. Get your message across in two or three words and perhaps use a tasteful image representation. I would advise the focus be on a unique logo identity as opposed to a banner. If you want to get a message across for that specific time frame - do it fast, furious, funky and with style.

4.   **Reciprocal linking and search engine strategies**

You may also be tempted to provide a link to your site in return for displaying a link to another's. This is similar to banner advertising in that a banner is also perceived as a linking type 'click here!' function. They say it can help you greatly with 'link popularity,' which is defined as one of the criteria used by most of the major search engines.

But let's indulge in a little bit of reality here! If you were to sit and submit your URL to the many, even thousands, of those major search engines, you would have to allocate a lifetime! It needs dedication and months of continuous re-submitting! Sure, there are those that would happily pay for a perceived 'platinum software' solution in order to guarantee a listing, but in the top what? The top 20? The top 50? The top 100? Truth has it that a search, regardless of those funky keywords, will find those multi-national organisations that have paid top dollar to be listed in the top rankings. What good is a 1,000th ranking (and I'm being kind here!) to you? How many surfers do you know trawl through to the 1,000th search page?

If you insist on ranking then be prepared to pay money to get there. To get priority listing on search engines is something to leave to the professionals. The web tools that promise to do this for you are pretty tame and useless. Far better to spend your time and money promoting your site OFFLINE. Put your web address in all your ads, business cards, letterheads, promotional fliers and logos. (Put it on the side of your car, van, bike, etc.). It is far better to lead people to the site than hoping people get to you by accident.

Alternatively, reciprocally link your site to those organisations that are affiliated in some way with you offline. That's assuming they have a web presence!

5.   **Traditional advertising**

Use traditional means to promote your site. This may seem surprising but if you are serious about 'driving traffic' to your site, it's no use relying on search engines (as most books tell you to do).

There are web tools you can buy which purport to help you to get onto the top pages of a search engine. These include statistics trackers, hits counters, a link watch and meta-tag generators. In reality, they are tedious tools. If you have the time and decide to implement these web technologies, then be prepared to spend the time making them work for you. Yes, implement them, but don't focus on them as your primary means of advertising or monitoring. If you have a site, then you have a purpose! Focus on that purpose and then utilise the tools available! What works well for one might not work well for another.

What the experts think

Search engine submission, its associated keywords and meta-tag generators are now a thing of the past. The search engines are corrupt and no longer work, as they should. The software programs you can buy to track statistics and maintain your site's position (supposedly!) in a search engine's listing is just another ploy for you to buy and it is not worth it.

Tip

- Tell the world about your wonderful web site but don't rely on search engines to do this for you. Instead, use traditional means of marketing the site.

- Put your web address in all your stationery, including letterheads and business cards.

- Place ads in the appropriate media and make sure your domain name and URL are clearly visible.

- Organise public relations events in which your URL largely features.

The future now!

Grasping the ASP

Be prepared for the launch of new, sexy web technologies. Active Server Pages (ASP), for example, is the live creation of a self-updating page determined by your location. Got a webzine or online newspaper or catalogue that needs updating daily? Then ask your web builder about ASP.

ASP pages are powerful applications that you can utilise to update, maintain and change content regularly. For example, an online newspaper will use this facility. But this is not a simple technology and it needs masses of space on a web server.

These new and powerful technologies will also allow your site to be written in any world language. So if your Chinese clients or readers click on your site, they get the pages AND the updated China-relevant information. Clever isn't it?

To have the ability to update regular content for your site quickly and efficiently is now no longer a dream. Rumour has it that ASP's attempts to exceed the abilities of its competitors will mean fast and furious upgrades and improvements to its services, leading to more and more powerful applications available online!

To see great examples of this technology in action take a look north of the border at www.theherald.co.uk or www.msn.com.

Databases are structured collections of data. To create a site that interacts with the stored information in a database is an evolving technology and one that really excites web builders (sad as it may seem!). Database-led sites allow you to respond to the latest market changes and/or new developments in your business, client needs and so on. As the data changes, so will your site ensuring that it is always up to date. These database-driven sites are not for beginners but they are something you should ask your web builder about if you're in the kind of business or area that changes rapidly.

If you want to know more about database-driven sites or are tempted to build your own have a look at the popular URL http://hotwired.lycos.com/webmonkey/ backend/databases.

At a guess, by now you may have already chosen to allocate the project to a professional. The web has drastic effects on the information economy of today's world. Universal accessibility through HTML, XML, JAVA and all other browser languages that power the web are making it less of an accessibility issue but open up vast new possibilities.

Flash - What the experts think

Funky web technologies are amazing, they really are, and in particular is Flash. We have seen many great sites purely designed and constructed in Flash. The technology this amazing tool is built on and what it can do astounds me. It's new...still new, given designers are becoming more and more creative in adapting it to suit their needs. And it's an exciting challenge to work with. A popular combination of creativity, technology and funk! People either love it or hate it. I guess you could say we love it. If a Flash web site is designed and developed well, it is unique. On the other hand, if it's designed and developed poorly it will be your reputation on the line.

Simplicity and subtlety are the keys to a successful site. Remember, there are many factors to take into consideration when designing a site but think about our listed 21st century tips and your users will thank you later!

References

The World Wide Web Consortium (W3C) [online]. Available from www.w3.org.

Your resource for designing useable, useful and accessible web sites and user interfaces [online]. Available from www.usability.gov.

The Web Developers Resource [online]. Available from http://hotwired.lycos. com/webmonkey.

Piperoglou, S: *HTML with Style* [online]. Available from http://webreference. com/html.

Flashkit - A Flash Developer Resource Site [online]. Available from www.flashkit. com.

Flaunders, V: *Where you learn good web design by looking at Bad Web design* [online]. Available from www.webpagesthatsuck.com.

Index

More books available from Law Pack...

How to Make Money Online

Forget the high-profile dot com failures - there are businesses out there making money online. This guide includes what will and won't sell, how to avoid e-business mistakes, how to give website visitors the confidence to buy online, getting payments, security software and systems, digital certificates and e-signatures, selling advertising space, supplying content, and much more!

Code B604	ISBN 1 902646 76 2	PB
250 x 199mm	160pp	£9.99	Jan 2002

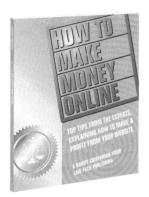

Online Marketing Strategies

What are your goals for your website? Is your website marketing you, or are you marketing it? And how will your website relate to your business's overall marketing strategy? This book provides guidance on building marketing into your website, on monitoring, evaluating and improving your internet or extranet site and on coordinating online and offline marketing strategies.

Code B602	ISBN 1 902646 75 4	PB
250 x 199mm	160pp	£9.99	Oct 2001

The Legal Guide to Online Business

Going online opens up a world of legal issues that can't be ignored. Domain names, trade marks, international jurisdictions, credit card transactions, partnerships, alliances, online contracts, employee email and internet policies and cyber crimes are some of the issues discussed and explained by specialist solicitor, Susan Singleton. Template documents included.

Code B603	ISBN 1 902646 77 0	PB
250 x 199mm	160pp	£9.99	Nov 2001

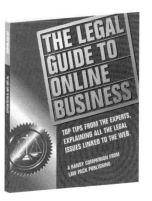

To order, visit www.lawpack.co.uk or call 020 7940 7000

More books available from Law Pack...

Limited Company Formation

Incorporation as a limited liability company is the preferred structure for thousands of successful businesses. *Limited Company Formation Made Easy* Guide explains why, and shows you how to set up your own limited liability company easily and inexpensively. It provides detailed but easy to follow instructions, background information, completed examples of Companies House forms and drafts of other necessary documents.

Code B503	ISBN 1 902646 43 6	PB
250 x 199mm	112pp	£9.99	1st edition

Profitable Mail-Order

Mail-order business is big business, and it's growing year by year. Setting up and running your own mail-order business can be fun as well as profitable. This *Made Easy* Guide shows you how to do it, explaining the vital importance of product profile, building valuable mailing lists, effective advertising and a whole lot more. It divulges the mail-order secrets that ensure success!

Code B510	ISBN 1 902646 46 0	PB
250 x 199mm	206pp	£9.99	1st edition

Running Your Own Business

You have a business idea that you want to put into action, but you also want advice on the realities of setting up and running a business: this *Made Easy* Guide is for you. It takes you through the business-creation process, from assessing your aptitude and ideas, to funding and business plans.

Code B511	ISBN 1 902646 47 9	PB
250 x 199mm	140pp	£9.99	1st edition